Religious Education of the Child

Copyright © 2005 The Light, Inc. & Işık Yayınları
Second Impression 2006

The Light, Inc.
26 Worlds Fair Dr. Suite C
Somerset, New Jersey, 08873, USA
www.thelightpublishing.com

Title	Religious Education of the Child
Author	M. Fethullah Gulen
Translation	Korkut Altay
Editor	Jane Louise Kandur
Art Director	Engin Ciftci
Published by	The Light, Inc.
Printed by	Caglayan A.S. - Izmir, 2006
ISBN	1-932099-28-X

Printed in Turkey

Publisher's Note: This book is a compilation from M. Fethullah Gulen's sermons "Family Education in Islam"..

Contents

1- Bringing up a Child with Multiple Abilities 7

2- Making our Children Familiar with Mosques at an Early age 9

3- Answering the Questions in the Child's Mind from the very Beginning 10

4- Worshiping and Praying within Sight of our Children 11

5- Respect for the Qur'an 15
    a) Not Causing our Children to Dislike Religion
    b) Continuing the Routine of Obligatory and Non-Obligatory Worship
    c) Respect for the Sacred Concepts

6- The Significance of Reading 26
    a) Reading and Writing
    b) Knowledge Leads to Awe of Allah
    c) Elimination of Doubts

7- Teaching about the Time of Happiness and Allah's Messenger (pbuh) 33

8- Introducing the Qur'an 36

9- Teaching about the Resurrection 37

Religious Education of the Child

Introduction

Marriage is a very serious affair in Islam and it must be dealt with due sensitivity. Couples planning to marry are not only future parents, but also future educators. Therefore, marriage should not be considered until a suitable age is reached for fulfilling this important mission.

Imam Ja'far required his disciples to delay their marriages. And Abu Hanifa did not allow his disciple, Imam Abu Yusuf, to marry for a certain period, telling him: "First you should complete your training and education, you should learn the subjects well that you need to learn before you marry. Otherwise, your education will be incomplete. Besides, you must have a job in order to support your family in a decent way. When you meet these conditions, your life path will be clearer." This is how Abu Hanifa preached to his young disciple - a disciple who attained the rank of Sheikh al-Islam during the Abbasid dynasty.

Abu Hanifa, the great figure who was known as the architect of theoretical law, chose to act in such a way. Imam Ja'far, who also taught not to rush into an early marriage, was one of the descendants of Allah's Messenger (pbuh). What we should understand from such advice is that the institution of marriage requires much thought and care. In this respect, when we are deciding whom to marry, we must ask ourselves the following questions: "Is this person competent to educate children as a teacher would? Do they seem mature enough to share a life with another? Are they well equipped to prepare children in accordance to our path?" If the spouses-to-be are able to answer all of these questions in the affirmative, then this means that they are ready for marriage. But if they are incapable of self-control, if they cannot get along with the people around them, if they cause problems everyday, then they cannot be said to be ready for marriage and raising children. Making an effective contribution to the future of Muslims - which should be the aim of every individual - depends on the existence of ideal individuals and ideal families. Such a lofty aim can only be realized by people whose hearts are as pure as the Ka'ba, whose worth is as great as Mount Everest, and whose spirituality extends as far as the lote-tree of the farthest limit (Sidrat al-Muntaha). It is not a task to be carried out by those who rebel against the Almighty with impure thoughts and corrupt consciences. Well-bred and enlightened generations who have reached inward and outward maturity will - by the Grace and help of Allah Almighty - realize this ideal. I would like to repeat what Allah's Messenger (pbuh) said when Habbab ibn Arat asked him to pray for victory: *"Allah will grant it, but what you need to do is fulfill the requirements of the causes"* (Bukhari, Manaqib, 25; Ikrah, 1).

These lines from the venerable Alvarli Efe[*] state beautifully what we are trying to say:

If your tears turn to a stream
If you cry like Ayyub did
If your heart truly grieves,
Will He not show any sympathy?

If you go near His door
Ready to sacrifice your dear life,
And serve as He ordered,
Will He not grant you a reward?

So, if our tears stream down and we exert ourselves in the search of new worlds to be discovered, we will receive good tidings at every resting place, we will sense the blessing of Allah each and every time, and we always keep walking toward Him without becoming entangled. This is the shape of our belief in the Almighty. We have absolute faith that He will prove us justified in our good intentions.

If parents want their children to exhibit certain types of behavior, it is of great importance that they practice such behavior themselves. In support of this, they must also be kind, affectionate and tender. In this way, homes turn into institutions of education.

[*] *Alvarli Efe (1866-1956) was a respectable Sufi scholar and one of Fethullah Gulen's teachers.*

1 – BRINGING UP A CHILD WITH MULTIPLE ABILITIES

If we want our children to be courageous, we should not frighten them with ideas of vampires, ghosts, giants, etc. We should raise them as strong individuals with a firm faith which will enable them to face up to any kind of difficulty.

If we really wish our children to have faith, all our attitudes and sensitivities in certain subjects, the way we go to bed and get up, the way we exert ourselves in prayer, the way we spread our affectionate wings over our children, must all reflect our faith in Allah and their hearts must be filled with such faith. We should always try to be the ideal for them, to avoid any kind of behavior which might make them feel contempt for us.

We should always try to maintain dignity and to remain elevated in their view, so that what we tell them will influence their hearts and they will not rebel against our wishes. In this respect, it can be said that a father who lacks seriousness can

probably be the friend of his children; but he can never be their teacher, and he will fail to bring them up the way he wants.

Our homes should always reflect the atmosphere of a temple and an educational unit at the same time; in this way we can satisfy our children's spirituality, their hearts and souls, thus we can save them from being slaves of their material desires.

2– MAKING OUR CHILDREN FAMILIAR WITH MOSQUES AT AN EARLY AGE

In the time of happiness,* children were free to go to the mosque at any time they wanted, no matter what age they were. It is a pity that nowadays we think that we will violate the sanctity of a mosque by taking children along. Likewise, it is such a pity that in many mosques we see elderly people shooing children away, frightening them.

---

* *The period corresponding to the lifetime of Prophet Muhammad (pbuh).*

Unfortunately, these narrow-minded people think that they are preserving the dignity of the mosque by frowning on the children's actions. In fact, what they are doing merely contradicts the tradition of Allah's Messenger (pbuh). He counseled Muslims that while standing in prayer in a mosque that the men should stand in front, then small boys, and then women and girls.

If this order of placement is followed, children will witness the pleasure and zeal of the adults at prayer; consequently, they will become more eager to practice their religion. Thus, rather than frightening them away, we should be trying to encourage them with small gifts, if possible, so that they warm toward prayer. We should make them love the mosques and their gardens, yet always strive to keep the sanctity of the mosque alive in their attitudes. When Allah's Messenger (pbuh) prayed in the mosque, he would take his granddaughter, Umamah, on his back, leaving her on the ground when he prostrated, and he would then take her on his back again before he stood up. This act is very important, as it is an example presented by Allah's Messenger (pbuh), the ultimate guide. The glorious Prophet (pbuh) never used an expression or held an attitude that could be considered harsh concerning the matter of children being taken to mosques. Therefore, a beautiful corner of our neighborhood should be spared for a mosque and our homes should be places of prayer; children will see aspects of life that will remind them of Allah in everything that they see around them; they will look at life in pious wisdom, they will choose their path and walk that way by their free will and conscience. Let us consider the prescribed prayers. When a child is old enough to pray, the father should hold his child's hand, take his child up to the prayer rug of the mother, inspiring spiritual depth and hearty devotion to Islam. Obtaining the expected result will be a great achievement, for prayers are of essential importance in terms of turning to Allah.

3– ANSWERING THE QUESTIONS IN THE CHILD'S MIND FROM THE VERY BEGINNING

Your children may have some questions concerning prayers and other religious matters. Introverted children are usually too shy to ask their parents such questions. However, it is of great importance that children open up and ask any questions on their minds concerning these subjects. If we leave such questions unanswered, then the questions will grow up alongside the child, and in the long run, doubts and hesitations will turn into a venomous snake that will poison their hearts.

Sometimes, these doubts in the inner world of a child can become such a rapid-growing wound that one day they could cause the spiritual collapse of our child, but we may not comprehend the situation until it is too late. The child may even seem to be praying with you at the mosque, saying *"There is no deity but Allah"*. In reality, however, such a child may have yielded to his inner conflict, and may be lost in a spiritual chaos. When we send our child to university in order that they will achieve social status and succeed to a bright future, it is inevitable that they will adopt some thoughts and attitudes that are incompatible with our religion, unless the child has had a proper spiritual background. From this point of view, the child should never be deprived of mental, emotional and spiritual back-up that is suitable to the child's age. In the past, children used to be entrusted to nannies. While looking after the children, these nannies would educate them spiritually as well, reaching into their inner world. In fact, this kind of education should be given to them by the parents themselves. If this cannot be, then they should ensure that this responsibility is fulfilled by a capable child-minder. In this way, parents will prevent their children from going astray. A firm belief, a sound consciousness of servanthood and perfected morality can only be realized through utmost sensitivity.

4– WORSHIPING AND PRAYING WITHIN SIGHT OF OUR CHILDREN

There should be a place and time for performing our prayers at home. We should either perform our prayers at home in congregation, if possible, or we should take our children to the mosque, holding their hands on the way. The latter option is actually more practical, especially if the mother cannot perform the prayers on certain days.[*] As she does not pray on these days, the children might think: *"I guess worship and prayer are optional."* That is why it would be a good idea to take our children to mosque particularly on these days. Yet, there is another way to eliminate such misunderstandings: On the days when women are not responsible for prayers, the mother may just perform ablution as usual, sit on the prayer rug, open her hands to the Almighty and pray to Him. If she does this, she

---

[*] *During menstrual period, etc.*

gains the merit of having performed the prayer as well as saving her children from possible misunderstandings. In Islamic reference books, this kind of behavior is also recommended. This is of essential importance in bringing up a child. When we act in this way, what the child sees around him or her will be prostrating heads, weeping eyes and hands open for praying. Your child will always be conscious of a servanthood fully recognized.

There will come a time when the adhan (call to prayer) is heard, and even if you do not hear the adhan, your child will warn you like an alarm clock, saying *"Dad/Mum, it's time to pray!"* You will thus reap the fruits of your labor.

In addition, you should spare time each day to pray to the Lord. At this time, a time previously determined, you should offer your prayers to the Almighty, invoking Him, thus practically demonstrating that the Exalted Creator can always be taken refuge in. It is better to pray aloud, openly. The companions of God's Messenger (pbuh) learned the supplications he recited while he prayed. Most of these were reported by his wife Aisha, but there are also similar reports from Ali ibn Abu Talib and his sons.

This clearly indicates that in order to teach your children how to pray, you should make your prayers heard by your children. If you wish your children to be sensitive people who tremble when Allah is mentioned, you, above everyone else, should present a practical example for them.

In my life, I have witnessed such scenes that I cannot help but tremble when I recollect them. The sight of my grandmother's devotion to the Lord had a great influence on me. When she passed away I was just a small child, but I still remember how she used to tremble as my father recited verses from the Qur'an or started talking about Islam. She was so sensitive about these matters that if you enthusiastically said *'Allah'* (may His glory be exalted) near her, she would immediately turn pale, and would remain thus the whole day. Her behavior had a great influence on me. In spite of being illiterate,

with a poor level of knowledge, her sincere prayers and genuine tears greatly influenced me. Many times, I have listened to learned people preaching enthusiastically, but none of them have affected me the way my grandmother has. It seems to me that I owe my being a Muslim to the sincerity of my parents and my grandmother.

So, parents should be careful of their acts in the home. As mentioned above, even the slightest pouring out of your worries to the Almighty, or moaning in supplication at His door, or praying openly in full submission to the Exalted Creator will affect your child more deeply than anything else. The memory of the efforts you made to ensure your afterlife, which is your greatest concern, will be imprinted on your child's mind and he or she will always remember you praying in hopeful awe. In fact, you must pray as if you see the Almighty, as if you are always in awareness of being in His presence. The way you stand, bow, prostrate and sit during the prayers should all recall Him. Your condition before Him can be pictured like this: Imagine yourself as if you were meeting Allah, as if He says: *"My servant! Stand up and account for your deeds in the world!"* and thus we stand submissively and respectively, in expectation of His Mercy. Such a state of praying, in which we feel His Sublimity and fully recognize our pettiness, is a genuine stimulant to all the people in the household, including ourselves. In a hadith (Prophetic saying) Allah's Messenger (pbuh) stated: *"I have such a moment with Allah that, at that very moment neither the angels of the highest rank nor any other creature can come close to me"* (Al-'Ajluni, Kashf al-Khafa, 2:173). So, should we have such a time, such an illuminated moment, and our children will be inspired from that moment of ours for their own prayers, when the time comes. In the future, whenever our children come up against a danger that may corrupt their faith and their worship, the memory of you praying will come to their rescue, like a guide to show them the way.

This fact should not be undermined, since in *sura* Yusuf, the Qur'an alludes to such a psychological fact. We know that the Prophet Yusuf was not a person to be tempted by a woman. However, the Qur'an states the following: *"... if it were not for a sign from his Lord"* (12:24).

Although a disputed fact, according to some of the greatest scholars who have expounded the Qur'an, the sign Yusuf saw was the image of his father Prophet Yaqub, who put his hand over his mouth and called out "Yusuf!" in astonishment. This event brought Yusuf to his senses, Yusuf who was a paragon of chastity, making him exclaim: *"Allah forbid!"* Your tearful eyes and sincere refuge in the Lord will play a vital role in your child's future life to help prevent a possible downfall. These will become such vivid pictures in the child's subconscious that your image will virtually be saying: *"My dear child, what are you doing!"* when they meet any kind of temptation, serving as a guide leading them away from various dangers.

5– RESPECT FOR THE QUR'AN

Reciting the Qur'an to your children and teaching them how to read it is of great importance, but there is something that is even more important. That is giving your children the sense that what is being recited is *"the word of Allah"*. Nowadays, one of the common problems we meet is that -unfortunately- the Qur'anic verses recited by some people just do not go beyond mere sound. If you can set a good example by reciting the Qur'an and do so as if you were reciting it before the Almighty Lord or beside the blessed soul of Allah's Messenger (pbuh), then you will have conquered the hearts of those around you once again. If you let your tears stream down your cheeks while you recite the Qur'an, your child will learn much. Reciting the Qur'an flatly may lead us to becoming insensitive.

A hadith declares the following: *"The person who recites the Qur'an most beautifully is the one who recites it in a solemn sadness."* Another hadith states: *"The Qur'an was revealed in a sad fashion"* (Ibn Maja, Iqama, 176; Zuhd, 19).

Given that the Qur'an deals with human beings, who have various worries (they surely do), we must reflect due sadness when we recite it. One of the most important points in attaining this level is to understand what the Qur'an is telling us. We must respect the Qur'an, for it is the word of Allah. If we make some efforts for a comprehensive understanding of its meaning, then this is an indication of further respect for it. Moreover, your child will feel the teachings of the Qur'an more deeply in his heart and mind, and in this way, he will satisfy his spiritual thirst to the extent that his level of understanding allows.

Those who do not study beyond the Qur'an can be considered as having a poor sense or understanding of religion. As for those who do not have even that slight connection with the Qur'an, they are at a total loss. Learning the deeper meanings of Qur'anic verses and teaching what we have learned to our children bear the utmost significance in terms of attaining the rewards promised by the Qur'an.

As an explanation of the hadith mentioned above, Hafiz Munawi narrates the following event: "A little boy was about to complete learning the Qur'an by heart. He spent the nights reciting the Qur'an and performing prayers, and in the morning he went to his teacher, pale and tired. His teacher was a great scholar and a true spiritual guide. He inquired of his students about that boy. His students replied: 'O master, that student of yours keeps on reciting the Holy Qur'an until the morning light without sleeping, and in the morning he comes to your lesson.' The master did not wish his student to recite the Qur'an in this manner, so he advised the following: 'The Glorious Qur'an must be recited in the same fashion as it was revealed, my son.' And he added 'From now on, you will recite it as if you are delivering what you learned to me.' The boy left and that night, he recited the Qur'an as his master had told him. In the morning, he went to his teacher and said, 'Sir, I only managed to recite the first half of the Qur'an.' His master said: 'Alright son, tonight, I want you to recite the Qur'an as if you are reciting it before Allah's Messenger (pbuh).' "

"This time, the student recited the Qur'an more carefully. He thought excitedly to himself: 'I am going to recite the Glorious Qur'an before the very person to whom it was revealed.' In the morning, he told his master that he was able to recite only a quarter of the Qur'an. On seeing the progress his student was making, the master elaborated the task step by step, as any good tutor would do, and he said: 'Now, this time you will recite the Holy Qur'an, imagining the moment when the blessed angel Gabriel revealed it to Allah's Messenger (pbuh).' The next day, the student came back and told his master: 'O master, I swear by Allah that I only managed to recite one *sura* last night.' And finally, his master said: 'My son, now recite it as if you are reciting before the Almighty Lord, Who is beyond thousands of veils. Think that Allah is listening to what you recite, following what He previously revealed for you.' In the morning, the student came to his master weeping: 'Master, I recited *'Praise be to Allah, the Lord of the worlds,'* and I went on until *'Master of the Day of Judgment'* but I just couldn't manage to say *'Only You do we worship.'* I just worship so many things, I bow in submission before so many things that I could not dare say *'Only You do we worship,'* when I imagined I was reciting it before The Lord.' "

Hafiz Munawi states that this boy did not live much longer and passed away a few days later. The wise spiritual trainer who helped him attain this level stood beside his grave, contemplating the young man in the Hereafter. Then, the boy called out from the grave: "O master, I am alive. I have attained such a spiritual rank that I was not called to account for my deeds."

Reciting the Glorious Qur'an by reflecting upon the meaning of the verses, considering every single word and showing due respect to Allah's word is vital for the opening up of our hearts; these genuine feelings draw both the one who recites it and the one who listens to the recitation into the blessed climate of the Qur'an, the gates of Heaven open wide.

By narrating this event, I am not trying to say that you should not recite the Qur'an unless you feel this way. On the other hand, paying due heed to what the Qur'an tells us is a necessity of being honored as His addressee. If Qur'anic verses do not effect great changes within our souls, then they cannot be expected to dominate our individual and social lives. We should be changed by the Qur'an, we should turn to Qur'anic horizons and keenly sense its depths; in this way will it open up its mysteries to the vision of our hearts.

Let us get back to the event we mentioned previously. That youngster did not die. He had merely returned to his Dear Lord. The excitement within his soul which was caused by the Qur'anic verses stopped his heart and he walked toward the Almighty. Surely, he would live forever. He had not been able to go beyond *"Only You do we worship"* so he kept repeating this until the dawn. Once, another person had the same experience while visiting the Ka'ba. When his head touched the wall of the Ka'ba, he said: "O, Lord!" and he just stopped spellbound... He was unable to go on any further, possessed by the thought: "Are you capable of saying that? Why don't you give up hypocrisy?" Nevertheless, what that man experienced can neither be expressed, nor can such a feeling be explained to other people. This is what he felt for a few moments. Even the man himself could not later explain his feelings.

In conclusion, if we maintain a certain attitude that reflects how devoted we are to the Qur'an and if our acts indicate our inclusion in the Prophet's circle, then our environment will rapidly bloom, just like green plants after a spring shower; there will be successive revivals and the angels will envy our life.

a) Not causing our children to dislike religion

In the recent past, the encouragement and instruction in points of our religion have not been properly conveyed to younger generations in Muslim countries. When we look at the situation with a pure heart and a sound mind, we will see that the underlying reason is ignorance and indifference about "meaning". Unfortunately, believers say: "We have faith in Allah" but they are not fully conscious of the meaning inherent in this statement. They are unable to maintain the coordination between the outer world and their inner worlds, and they fail to comprehend religious concepts correctly. This has been a recurring error throughout history.

Even now, we cannot say that we are making good use of the opportunities granted us by Allah. When our children come to us with questions concerning religion on their minds, our duty is to fill their hearts with the love of Allah and His Messenger (pbuh), rather than intimidating them by obliging them to memorize some prayers, prayers which if left to time, they will learn spontaneously in the future. If we feel content with teaching our religion as if it were only a set of formalities to be learned by heart, our children may end up feeling antagonized by our religion. After just one lesson, they may refuse to learn. We do not feed a six-month-old baby with adult food.

Likewise, we should not insist that children memorize until they are of age. Hopefully, they will try to learn what they should without being told to do so. Our approach should be based on making them love, think about and internalize Islam.

Believers must be sensitive to this subject and try to make religion as enjoyable as possible. They should try to open up their children's hearts and minds to spirituality. They should love the Qur'an so much that they would say "O, Almighty Allah! Grant me the ability to comprehend the religion, enable me to learn the divine purposes so that I shall be filled with Qur'anic truth" and their life will become centered around this perspective.

b) Continuing the routine of obligatory and non-obligatory worship

Parents should perform their religious duties properly, no matter what conditions prevail, so that their children will not see any lapse in their servanthood to the Lord. Allah's Messenger (pbuh) never abandoned performing *tahajjud* (night prayer) and he had particular prayers which he recited when he got up in the night. He would perform a "make-up" prayer whenever he missed the recitation of these prayers, even though they were not obligatory. In this way, he clearly demonstrated that any practice of worship at home or outside is never to be abandoned.

The companions of the Prophet (pbuh) were perfectly aware that once you commenced a practice of worship, you should continue in the same manner. 'Abd Allah ibn 'Amr ibn 'As, who was one of the ascetics of the time, wished to fast everyday and keep vigil at prayer every night until dawn. Furthermore, when he married, he kept away from his wife for days. When his wife complained to our Prophet (pbuh) through her father-in-law, 'Abd Allah ibn 'Amr ibn 'As had to go to Allah's Messenger (pbuh) and he was reprimanded for neglecting his wife. That day, Allah's Messenger (pbuh) wanted him to reduce his supererogatory worshiping; yet he insisted on worshiping more and said: "O Allah's Messenger (pbuh), I am capable of performing more." In the end, Allah's Messenger (pbuh) convinced him to fast every second day, to sleep for one third of the night and to keep vigil for the rest. Later, this blessed companion said to another, as reported in Bukhari and Muslim: "I wish I had agreed with what Allah's Messenger (pbuh) had told me. It is so difficult to keep up such practices at this old age. Nevertheless, I don't want to abandon the supererogatory worshiping I have been performing. I want Allah's Messenger (pbuh) to find me exactly as he left me."

'Abd Allah ibn 'Amr ibn 'As is a good example; one should not abandon habitual worship. Allah's Messenger (pbuh) stated that *"The most meritorious kind of worship is the one that is performed steadily, even if it is of little amount"* (Bukhari, Tahajjud, 7). If you cannot do much, stick to what you can and perform such prayers regularly, so that your child will form a good opinion of you. If you can only perform the obligatory and the *sunna* (the Prophet's traditions) prayers, you should perform them thoroughly. If you have begun to perform any kind of supererogatory prayer (*Tahajjud, Awwabiyn, Duha,* etc.), you should continue to do so. Otherwise, your child may wonder why you are neglecting them. Through keeping a steady habit of worship, the subconscience of your child will be dominated by positive views on prayer.

So far, what we have discussed appeals to those who share our way of thinking. This is the path we need to choose, if we are to bring up our children as sensitive, pious and learned Muslims. Every aim is achieved through a particular method. In order to enable our children to attain happiness in this world and in the Hereafter, our method should be to set them a practical example. All this may sound like some complicated prescription, but it is not that difficult to carry out.

c) Respect for the sacred concepts

There are certain concepts that bear utmost sanctity. Belief in Allah is a pillar of Islamic faith. One who does not believe in Allah cannot be said to have an Islamic life or faith. We should keep in mind that the conquest of our children's hearts by these exalted and sacred notions is our responsibility when they come of age (usually the ages between 7 and 9 is considered an ideal time). Ensuring that a child lives with the remembrance of Allah's Messenger (pbuh) can be achieved by talking about Allah at home, every now and then. If your primary topic of conversation is the celebrities who appear on TV, then these people will naturally dominate the imagination of your child. He will tell you the names of various movie stars, sportsmen, musicians and other celebrities easily, but he will be unable to memorize even a few of the names of the companions of our

Prophet (pbuh). His memory and subconscious will be occupied by useless things.

Our actions must reflect due respect for anything sacred to us. The Ka'ba for instance, is a sacred place. When you express your feelings about the Ka'ba near your child, you should be very respectful. When we step into the borders of the Ka'ba or approach Madina, our feet should touch the ground with full respect. We should even go so far as to say -as did Imam Malik - "This is not a place to go ride or walk with shoes." Whenever that great *imam* reached the borders of Madina, coming from a long distance to teach hadith at al-Masjid an-Nabawi or another mosque, he would dismount and say that this was the way one should act within that city. Naturally, any child who observes this kind of behavior will overflow with respect for the owner of Ar-Rawda.*

The same goes for the Glorious Qur'an. The Qur'an states: "...and he who venerates the sacred rites of Allah - it is the fruit of the piety of the hearts" (22:32). The source of the veneration of the sacred rites is piety of the heart. Piety of the heart is to be attained through the heart's recognition of Allah, by turning to Him in respect, by taking refuge in Him, by obeying Him and by discerning the Divine Truth. This kind of veneration is of vital importance. Mosques, for instance, will have such an exalted place in the child's mind that he will think all the roads to Allah start from the mosques.

When the beautiful voices of the muezzins call out from minarets, saying "Allahu akbar", your child should echo the words of the *adhan*, and when it is over, they should open their hands and recite the *adhan* prayer (O Allah! Lord of this perfect call and of the salat to be performed, grant our Master Muhammad (pbuh) nearness to Haqq, reaching Heaven and beyond; and elevate him to the *Maqam al-Mahmood* (The Praised Position) which You have promised him).

---

* *The place between Prophet Muhammad's tomb and the pulpit of his mosque which is called "a Garden from the Gardens of Paradise" as reported in a hadith (Fath al-Bari, 1888).*

In conclusion, if we nurture love for Allah, if we really have feelings of respect for the essentials of Islam, then we should convey these feelings to our children's hearts, show them the greatness of Allah, make them love Him and take His love very much to heart, so that our children will see that there is no one else to be truly loved, sought for or longed for other than the Absolute Lord. In a hadith which Tabarani reported to have been narrated by Abu Umama, Allah's Messenger (pbuh) stated: *"Make Allah's servants love Allah, so that Allah will love you"* (Munawi, Fayd al-Qadir, 3:371). Allah can be loved only by being familiar with Him; human beings are friendly to what is familiar and hostile to what is strange. Pagans or atheists are hostile to Allah because of their ignorance of Him. If such people knew Him well they would love Him. In the Qur'an Allah decrees: *"I have not created the jinn and mankind except to worship Me"* (51:56). Ibn Abbas and Mujahid interpret the expression *"except to worhip Me"* as 'so that they become familiar with Me', which means if one is familiar with Allah, then one is fulfilling one's duty as a servant; if not, then one is ungrateful to one's Lord.

So, first of all we should make a child familiar with Allah, then the child's heart will be full of His love and they will pay due respect to Him. There must be a particular way of introducing Allah, a way which suited to the age of the child. Merely stating the fact that the dinner on the table comes from Him can be sufficient to make our point. At an older age, it would be wise to tell the child that the rain, which all humans, animals and plants need, pours down from the sky by the Grace of Allah; the showers which enliven the earth overflow from His treasures of Mercy. To an older child, we need to tell more about intricate physical facts, such as how evaporation takes place, how rain pours down in tiny drops, and explain why none of these cannot be the result of pure coincidence; we need to tell them that everything takes place through His bestowal. As for children of further discernment, you can tell them about Allah, using factual support put forward by contemporary science.

Once Allah's Messenger (pbuh) stated the following: *"Love Allah for He grants blessings to you; love me, for I am His Messenger; and love my family for you love me"* (Tabarani, 3:46).

It is not difficult to make your children love Allah's Messenger (pbuh) and his companions, so long as you find the right method. If we give them the blessed life story of the Prophet (pbuh) to read instead of more frivolous books, or at least provide them with Yusuf Kandahlawi's *Hayat al-Sahaba* (Life of the Companions) which is a very good reference book, then they will have a chance to learn about our Prophet, his companions and about the children of the companions. In this way, each of these blessed people will have a high place in our children's view; they will be aching to be as courageous as Hamza ibn 'Abd al-Muttalib, as strong as Ali ibn Abu Talib, as truthful as Abu Bakr Siddiq and as just as Umar ibn al-Khattab.

It is of utmost significance that the Qur'an, the life story of our Prophet (pbuh) and other books on the life of his companions have a place of honor at home; our children's hearts will be saturated with and illuminated by our historical figures.

I would like to draw your attention to an important point here. Although using different arguments against philosophical theses and notions that threaten our faith is a logical reaction, merely dealing with just logic can damage our spiritual life and lead us to despair. After having grasped a logical explanation, your child will want to see some practical examples. Even if you climb up a beautiful ladder descending from heavens with thousands of proofs from macro - and micro - cosmoses for the existence and oneness of Allah, if you fail to give practical examples from life, your child will find all these proofs too theoretical and difficult to comprehend; he might perceive the religious thought that you were trying to present as nothing more than some obscure philosophical view.

If you do not make it clear that what you are talking about really took place at a certain period in history, it may just sound like a fairy tale. This is why we have to show children that certain principles were put into practice in the past and can be put into practice again.

Until quite recently, it has sometimes been said: "What is said about the companions may be true, but probably this has only happened once and it is nearly impossible for such things to happen again." Such negative thoughts were like an epidemic. However, when we see the young people today who know the Exalted Creator and His Glorious Messenger (pbuh) and who love them deeply, then we can believe that there can again be a community whose lifestyle resembles that of the companions. Considering the hints and glad tidings given in the Qur'an and supported by the Hadith, we can have faith in the advent of a community described by Allah's Messenger (pbuh) as being the *"gharibs"*, the people who are regarded as strangers in their own land because of their belief and lifestyle who will present Islam's exalted values.

The piety in your heart, the love and veneration you have for Allah, your respectful acts toward mosques and the sacred rites will seem to a child as radiant signs that invite him to Allah's path.

Adhan (the call to prayer) is a symbol of Islam and a means of concentration before the prayers. At the same time, adhan is an invitation from Allah to His servants to fulfill their duties, a reminder of His Greatness. If you manage to bring up your children with such feelings in their hearts, whenever they hear the adhan, they will be on the verge of tears, moved, excited and full of love for the Lord; they will tremble like a leaf. In spite of all misfortunes, this sacred duty was properly carried out by previous Muslims and -Insha Allah (if Allah wills)- it will be carried out again with the same effectiveness in the near future. We will teach new generations to pay due homage to the pillars of Islam, we will teach everyone to love Allah and His Messenger.

To sum up, our religious duties should be thoroughly fulfilled at home; any doubts or hesitations concerning our religion and faith in our children's minds should be eliminated as early as possible. In addition, there should be certain times of the day when we strive to attain the ultimate intimacy with the Almighty, turn to Him in supplication and full of hope, as Divine Mercy pours down on us in abundance and our hearts overflow with sadness. In such a time as this, the presence of Allah's Messenger (pbuh) will be felt in the home through the behavior of the master and the mistress.

The values your child will acquire in this way are so great and priceless that in his future life he will enjoy the fruits of your efforts and pray for you in gratitude.

Respecting the sacred pillars means to accept and display the greatness of values that are held dear by Islam. The love of the Most Exalted One will blossom in young hearts with *"Allahu akbar"* during adhan, this love will wave like a flag in their spiritual worlds, it will possess their hearts completely and you will be gratefully smiling in return for these divine blessings.

6– THE SIGNIFICANCE OF READING

One of the most important subjects in educating your child is "reading and writing". Teaching our children how to read and write should be oriented toward a goal, rather than simply for the sake of learning. They should not want to be led, but rather promote themselves to the level of a guide. To know why you read is as important as reading itself.

Let us think about the following questions: "What is knowledge? What is the purpose of knowledge? Why do people read books? What is the target that we desire to reach by reading and understanding something?"

If a person learns the complex and confusing rules and principles of mathematics, but ignores their practical applications or never thinks of improving their knowledge with theories and hypotheses, then they cannot be considered as having realized their goal.

Likewise, if we learn all the basic principles of medicine, but do not put this knowledge to use, not even examining a single patient, it is doubtful whether we will be able to keep up our knowledge, not to mention the fact that we have wasted our knowledge.

In short, knowledge in which we do not find anything that relates to ourselves or to someone else is, obviously, of no use to anyone.

a) Reading and writing

It is an accepted fact that a major priority established by the Qur'an is reading and writing. However, I would like to emphasize that just filling up your memory without trying to discern the divine purpose is not commendable. We should take a child by the hand, let their soul enjoy the Qur'an and arouse their interest in the Qur'an. Thus, in the future, that child will try to discern what Allah demands from us. Unfortunately, we think that we have done enough by merely telling the child to say "Bismillah". In fact, "Bismillah" is very important, and it consolidates faith. On the other hand, there is a matter of further importance. That is, we must teach the Divine Purposes (no matter how briefly); these are what must be taught and learned above all else. There are several glorious periods in our history. In a certain period, there were some governors, judges and jurists who knew the Qur'an by heart in every Muslim country. However, these people did not grasp the essence of what they were studying, rather they just copied those who had preceded them, unable to put forth any fresh comments on scientific or religious matters. They lacked the ability to make sound judgments.

There came a time when these narrow-minded people, who clung to their insufficient knowledge, persisted in committing sins by keeping silent about some methods and principles that contradicted our religion. Naturally, these people failed to preserve the dignity and honor of Islam. Unfortunately, their efforts mocked our people and our religion. Their knowledge was not internalized nor did it guide their hearts. The Qur'anic verse *"...and whomever He leads astray - those are the losers"* (7:178) is explained as follows, in a Hadith, reported by Huzayfa ibn al-Yaman to Hafiz Abu Ya'la: *"One of the things I worry about you is that a person who reads the Qur'an so much reflects the brilliance of the Qur'an in all their behavior. Islam becomes a dress for them. They are clad with this dress until the time appointed by Allah comes. Then, all of a sudden - may Allah protect them - they take off that dress and abandon it. They approach their brothers brandishing their sword, accusing them of shirk (associating partners with Allah)."* Huzayfa asked: *"O Allah's Messenger (pbuh), who is nearer to shirk; the one who is accused of shirk or the one who accuses of shirk?"* Allah's Messenger (pbuh) answered: *"The one who accuses of shirk"* (Ibn Kathir, Tafsir al-Qur'an, 3:59).

Even today, there are so many people with important titles who live in sheer ignorance, who neither know Allah nor His Messenger (pbuh). The ones who fail to reflect on the thousands of verses and proofs in the universe, the ones who are indifferent to the facts and events around them are absolutely ignorant, no matter what their titles are. Since what we acknowledge as 'knowledge' is the knowledge which illuminates the mental and spiritual worlds of an individual, the other types of knowledge are just burdens on our brain.

The first command of the Qur'an is *"Read, in the name of your Lord…"* Allah does not say "read the Qur'an"; He does not say "Read what has been revealed to you." The Qur'an itself explains the meaning of the order *"Read"* and draws attention to creation by saying: *"Read, in the name of your Lord, Who created" (96:1)*. Here, there is also an allusion to recognizing the signs of Allah on the face of creation.

"Read, by your Most Generous Lord, Who taught by the pen" (96:3-4).

As we see, reading and writing are mentioned successively. So, humans will read and write; but whatever they read, they will read with the aim of discerning their innermost faculties, the essence of the Qur'an and sensing the divine power beyond the creation and the laws of the universe. From time to time, they will look into their own physiology and anatomy; sometimes they will observe the creation. As a result, they will convey the spiritual outcome of their reflection to others, beginning with their own family.

The subsequent verses suggest what is meant by the order *"Read"* is not merely reading Qur'anic verses. By ordering us to read, the Qur'an counsels us to read divine commands, to comprehend the aim of creation and to discover the laws of the universe. Therefore, when we read, we are supposed to reflect upon the creation of human beings, the laws of the universe and the Revelation in Allah's name. The Qur'an raises the question "How were we created?" by mentioning creation. Right after this, the Qur'an directs our thoughts to the mystery of creation by saying that we are created from an *"alaq"* (clot), which is described as a drop of water in another verse.

Allah who orders us to read the book of the universe along

with the Qur'an, presents human beings with such a lesson that everyone - from an ordinary person of the lowest level of discernment to the most distinguished thinker - will learn from this lesson to the extent that their capacities allow.

The Qur'an also mentions *"the pen"*, which implies writing: *"Nun. By the pen and what they inscribe…"* (68:21). After the initial (muqatta'a) letter, Allah begins the *sura* by taking an oath upon the pen, clearly indicating the emphasis He places on writing.

This pen can be the pen of the angels who keep a record of our deeds, the pen which has written down our destinies, or it can be the pen you use at school or somewhere else, it doesn't make any difference. The person who uses the pen makes the difference, and Allah's oath upon the pen involves everything we have mentioned.

b) Knowledge leads to awe of Allah

In another verse, it is stated that: *"Indeed, of His servants, only the learned fear Allah"(35:28)*. Indeed, only the learned are truly respectful of Allah, since the sense of respect in divinity depends on knowledge. The ones who do not know Allah and who are ignorant of the mystery of divinity obviously lack due respect and awe.

Starting off from this point of view, if we want to raise our children well, one of the most important things to do is to instill in the child a firm belief. They should also be informed, as much as possible, about the proofs of the Almighty Lord's existence. Sometimes, such proofs might eliminate your doubts, but they can be difficult to understand for a child. If this is the case, then other approaches should be tried.

Another important point is to conquer their hearts with love for the Prophet (pbuh). In order to realize this, we need to tell them about his life.

c) Elimination of doubts

Nowadays, we come up against many questions like "Who has created the universe?" or -Allah forbid - "Who has created Allah?" The commonness of such questions indicates that children have not been given a satisfactory explanation concerning Allah. The underlying reason behind the question "Why did the Prophet (pbuh) have more than one wife?" is just the same. The child who asks this question does not have proper information concerning Allah's Messenger (pbuh).

Likewise, some people make comments like: "Allah's Messenger (pbuh) was a very intelligent man. The changes he made were the results of his intelligence." Obviously, these people lack religious education and they are not aware of the real meaning of "Prophethood".

Moreover, if there arises misinformation from society, this just makes matters worse. We should feed the spiritual world of our child with healthy ideas, so that in the future they will have a firm belief. If what you tell a child is appropriate for the age of that child, then it will be convincing for them. In this way, you will have eliminated some possible doubts that may have arisen in their minds.

Once the Zoroastrians (fire-worshippers) asked Abu Hanifa some questions, and demanded satisfactory answers. They told Abu Hanifa that they did not believe in Allah, at a period when both scientific progress and Islamic thought were on the rise. There were many Zoroastrians in Kufah, the city where Abu Hanifa lived.

Abu Hanifa explained everything to them in a very simple way: "If you saw a boat heading with ease for the shore in a rough sea, expertly steered and keeping a steady course, in spite of the waves, would you doubt that there is somebody on board, steering it with perfect skill?" They replied in chorus: "No, we wouldn't!" Then the great *imam* asked: "So, these stars, this vast universe, the earth steer easily through the sea on a steady course; how can you think that all this happens on its own?" On hearing this, the Zoroastrians said: "La ilaha illa'llah Muhammadan Rasulullah."

Here, what he did was to make the explanation suit the level of the people he was addressing. For some, this may be too simplistic, while for others it may be sufficient. No matter how logical such an explanation is, after a certain age is reached, it will no longer suffice. When the time comes, we need to make the argument with ideas that require deeper thought. We can give various examples using the universe, human biology, etc. The human body, its inner mechanisms, its cells, systems, anatomy and physiology are all created to an amazing degree of perfection. In my opinion, introducing these examples within a scientific framework will help us to achieve the desired effect. We can also talk about the various features of air, water, light, vitamins, proteins, carbohydrates or microorganisms. Actually, only the presentation will differ; it is merely the continuation of the same lesson. The way Bediuzzaman Said Nursi* spoke of Allah is a very good example of what we have said: "Every village must have its headman. Every needle must have its manufacturer and craftsman. And, as you know, every letter must be written by someone. How then, can it be that so extremely well-ordered a land should have no ruler?" Asking how the universe, so vast and magnificent, can be left unattended and asking how things can happen on their own is a good method to get a child to start thinking. If we go through the available publications on this subject, we can obtain plenty of material. All we need to do is to pick out the right subjects for the young people we are addressing.

7– TEACHING ABOUT THE "ERA OF HAPPINESS" AND ALLAH'S MESSENGER (PBUH)

We must be very sensitive about introducing Allah's Messenger (pbuh). The fact that some people dislike Allah's Messenger (pbuh) nowadays can be attributed to the fact that they were not informed about him during their childhood. The ones who knew him well admire and adore him. Throughout the centuries, masses of people, fascinated by his charm, have followed him, and no man in the world history has been thus respected. However, we cannot expect our children to love Allah's Messenger (pbuh) without telling them about him. At a certain time period, there was a fortunate group of people who had the honor of seeing and being with him. Another fortunate group saw the ones who saw him and tried to see him through the eyes of the preceding generation. This is summed up in the hadith:

"The best among you (are) the people (who belong to) my age. Then those next to them ..." (Muslim, Fada'il al-Sahaba, 210).

---

* *A famous Turkish Islamic scholar (1877-1960) who wrote the Risale-i Nur Collection, a modern Qur'anic commentary.*

Allah's Messenger (pbuh) came at a very dark time; at that time there were heartless people who buried their daughters alive, almost everyone drank alcohol and there was a very weak moral code. Such a blessed person, one who accomplished an incredible social reform, all of his achievements and his community are absolutely peerless throughout all of history.

Some revolutions took place in Ancient Greece, Rome and in other countries also. However, none of these offered much in terms of human values. These revolutions brought new problems and in some places there was a return to the past. We can even say that in certain periods, what was left behind by revolutions was nothing but blood and tears.

A real revolution is one which effects positive changes within the hearts, the souls, the social and spiritual life, the feelings and thoughts of the people; one which frees them from the grasp of the carnal self and elevates them to the top of humanity, resulting in a chain of pure generations. This is what Allah's Messenger (pbuh), the greatest expert on social life, achieved as a Prophet, thanks to his excellent ability at dealing with social matters. Unfortunately, we have neglected to learn about him and to convey any knowledge about him to our children, although he set an ideal example in every aspect of life.

Here is another point from Bediuzzaman Said Nursi: "A little habit, like cigarette smoking in a small community can only be removed permanently by a powerful ruler, and only with great effort." To paraphrase this: If ten people try to persuade a heavy smoker to give up smoking, telling him how it causes cancer in a most convincing manner, they will still not be able to make him give up smoking. On the other hand, Allah's Messenger (pbuh) abolished all the evil habits of the people around him, something which seemed impossible at the time, replacing these with the most exalted human values.

The incredible obedience to the prohibition of alcohol was a remarkable fact. Imagine an alcoholic community, where alcohol is a part of life. As soon as they heard the order "alcohol is prohibited", they smashed the glass in their hand, never to drink again. Academics have failed to explain how this reform has been so effective. Thus, what we need to do is to learn about this blessed person who had the greatest virtue and to speak about what we know of him to others, so that his love will conquer their hearts. When we achieve this, our children will speak about him, think about him and they will sense him. As a result, we will have direct back up in our efforts from Allah's Messenger, Muhammad (pbuh). May the Almighty consolidate our faith through this blessed person!

Telling our children about Allah's Messenger (pbuh) and all the events he foretold will refresh their trust in him. In his hadiths, he foretold many events that would happen in the future, including their causes and their results, stretching from his time until the end of the world, and warned us about these events.

He foretold several events, such as the Mongolian invasion, the occupation of Syria, the tremendous increase in the value and importance of the river Euphrates, petroleum being found in Taleqan, the spread of corrupt morality and so on. It is virtually impossible to deny his Prophethood when one is aware of all these facts. It is our responsibility to let others know that Allah's Messenger (pbuh) revealed the knowledge of both the past and the future, despite the fact that he had never received any education, except that given by Allah.

He stated facts concerning medicine that would later prove to be true, even though at that time it was impossible for him to know such facts from the basic level of scientific knowledge of those times. Therefore, Allah taught him and he revealed what he had been taught, clearly indicating that he was truly Allah's Messenger (pbuh). If we were to prepare a serious study concerning his deeds, volumes of books would not suffice. We have briefly mentioned some facts.

8– INTRODUCING THE QUR'AN

Making younger generations love the Qur'an is of great importance when trying to raise their religious consciousness. Merely saying "the Qur'an is sacred" is too superficial a statement to describe the Qur'an, and to introduce it to a child. Such an attitude might seem to be appropriate at times, but it is sure to fall short in the long run; it is even harmful in that it leads to a future prejudice against religious teaching. From this point of view, we should tell and convince the child that the Qur'an is the latest and indisputable revelation from Allah, with decisive judgments pointing to the farthest limits of science and technology.

In fact, the Qur'an is a wonderful book which confirms all the latest scientific findings concerning the universe, creation and existence. It even gives concise data about such subjects. We can say that it explains everything from the micro to the macro scale in terms of servanthood. The following verse confirms this point:

"With Him are the keys of the unseen; only He knows them, and He knows what is on land and in the sea. Not a leaf falls but He knows it; and there is no grain in the dark bowels of the earth, nor anything green or dry, but is (recorded) in a Clear Book" (6:59).

9– TEACHING ABOUT THE RESURRECTION

Our next step should be to talk about the resurrection. The child should believe in their hearts that as soon as this life ends, a new life, an everlasting afterlife, will begin. Science, wisdom and reality point out that Allah created this universe and that

He maintains it. He is the One Who demonstrates and fixes 'time'. The Qur'an alludes to this fact by the following verse:

"Say: Travel in the land and see how Allah originated the creation; then Allah produces the other generation. Allah truly has power over everything" (29:20).

Therefore, we should investigate the laws of the universe, examine everything step by step; we should see and reflect on how life began on earth, how this universe came into existence out of nothing, how human beings appeared, how various forms of life were created as different species and how perfection was completed with human beings.

Allah, Who created the universe from nothing, will certainly resurrect us. Is the One Who has established this order not able to establish another? Is the One Who created this earth so splendidly not able to create another? Can He not call this world as 'worldly life', and the other one as 'the Hereafter'? Can the One Who brought us to this world not take us to an eternal abode? Such explanations are at a suitable level for the comprehension of our children.

We can see that the skies and the earth have been created perfectly with our eyes. Like a fish swimming in the sea, or a bird soaring in the sky, those immense systems, those nebulas float by so smoothly in an enrapturing harmony through the universe, that no disorder or randomness can be seen by one who looks with eyes of wisdom. Moreover, this harmony is explicit even to the simplest mind. The Glorious Qur'an highlights all of these and points to the special significance of the creation of humans, apart from the creation of the heavens and the earth.

"Allah, Who created the heavens and the earth in six days, sat upon the Throne. You have no guardian or intercessor, apart from Him. Do you not recollect?" (32:4).

"Who fashioned well everything He created, and originated the creation of man from clay" (32:7).

The Glorious Qur'an says Allah created and ordered these magnificent systems. He will create a different universe after they have been demolished. These are undeniable facts. There are a lot of unique and crystal clear statements on this subject contained in the Glorious Qur'an.

In the following verse, the Glorious Qur'an addresses those who deny resurrection: *"Say: 'He Who originated them the first time will bring them back to life and He has knowledge of every creation'"* (36:79).

Another verse decrees: *"Behold, then, the marks of Allah's Mercy, how He revives the earth after it was dead. He, indeed, is the One Who revives the dead and He has power over everything"* (30:50).

The Glorious Qur'an's articulate style, free from redundancy, will explain what needs to be told to people of every age very clearly. The Archangels and destiny are also among subjects that need to be regarded sensitively. We must make it very clear to the younger generation in different ways that everything has a program, a project, and a plan; thus so must the universe. This program called 'destiny' is within divine knowledge and it includes everything that has not come into existence yet.

In conclusion, we will have shown our children the *"Sirat al-Mustaqim"* (the right path) only after having taught all these things to them; we will have said *"Lead us to the right path"* (1:6) both in words and actions. *Insha Allah*, we will reap the benefit of our efforts and of our practical prayer by the Grace of the Almighty Lord. By teaching our children everything from the essentials of faith to the pillars of Islam, we should direct them to the Almighty, and in this way, we will save them from mental and spiritual death.

If children grows up in a pure atmosphere, *Insha Allah* their spirituality will not be shaken by any evil they face and they will always be obedient servants of Allah.

NOTES